Gemini/Scorpio/Capricorn

By Shay Caroline Simmons, Kelli Simpson, and Joy Ann Jones

Copyright © 2013 Shay Simmons, Kelli Simpson and Joy Ann Jones

All rights reserved.

ALL CAPS PUBLISHING

P.O. Box 368

Easthampton, MA 01027

USA

ISBN-10: 0615771084
ISBN-13: 978-0615771083

DEDICATION

Dedicated to the loves of our lives:

Bosco, who herds Shay Caroline tirelessly

Big Snoop, who subdues Kelli's offending oven mitt

and Chinook, who bravely chases away the demons for Joy.

CONTENTS

Acknowledgments   I

1   Poems by Shay Caroline   1

2   Poems by Kelli Simpson   42

3   Poems by Joy Ann Jones   81

4   One Form, Three Poets   113

ACKNOWLEDGMENTS

Joy Ann Jones wishes to thank Prime J, without whose encouragement 400 poems would never have been written.

"The Red Shoes" appeared in Annell Livingston's book The Red Shoes Artists Book Project, lulu press.

Shay Caroline wants to thank Kelli, my Favorite from the start, and Joy, my dearest friend in the world. Also, Lou Fisher, who helped me discover what I could really do with words.

Kelli says, some poems from this collection have previously appeared in Curio Poetry.

Many thanks to Shay and Joy for all of the support, snark, and sisterhood.

And, to my little girl: see, this is what Mama does when she's playing on the computer!

1. POEMS BY SHAY CAROLINE

"The Girl Who Liked Hemingway"

I didn't win the pageant
because those bitches wouldn't know beauty if it beat them over their 'do's
with a porch plank.

My Mediterranean sultriness was not what they were looking for;
them with their politeness and their narrow-lipped smiles holding back the
churning reflux that their hearts produce.

They are not human.

As a baby, I was different.
I spoke within minutes, asking for a mirror before milk,
and sharing Portuguese brandy with my father in the library before the
month was out.

Let others become checkers at Target.
Let others slave in the shamba under a broiling sun.
They do not have my sculptured cheekbones,
and so must scramble and struggle while I laze under an awning in a cafe,
accepting the dazzled worship of waiters named Jean-Guy.

But look, it hasn't been all roses and honey, just the same.
I stayed barefoot until I was twelve, by choice.
I whipped all the local boys,
and was the terror of the American compound.

I first considered pageants when I was caught siphoning gas from a diplomat's car.
(I had wanted to burn down Amber Rae's house; I didn't like her.)
The diplomat took me inside and stood with his back to me,
gazing through his wife's sheer curtains at the stucco buildings across the street, and said,

"There are other things
you could be doing."

Soon I was shivering,
my arm dangling boneless over the edge of the dining room table,
smiling at the patterned copper ceiling.
I had still been in command of myself when he lost all his polish and said
things to me that were not diplomatic, but rather,
the shouts of a drowning man finding shore.

So anyway,
these bitches looked at me critically, as if I were a steer at auction,
each of them a little complacent fat cask of petty.
I knew I couldn't win,
and my mind turned, as it always has,
toward ways to rain down destruction upon my enemies' heads.

I have a little French *cahier*
that I write down my dreams and plans in.
If the gendarmes ever find it, I'm so fucked.

But never mind.
The world of pageants plateaus early--
one is done at twenty, turned loose in the streets to blink big-eyed
at the onrushing autobus that will flatten you dead.
Does this sound like me?
Does it?

I am a girl who will never need a raincoat,
because it never dares to rain on my perfect creamy shoulders.
I own no pearls,
but I have six different sets of Ben Wa balls,
one for each day of the week, and then I go to Mass on Sunday.

I didn't win the pageant,
but I escaped to Algiers and met a man.

In the morning, we start out together for Kilimanjaro--
I shall be barefoot, in my element once more,
and McComber will have some sort of accident and leave everything to me.

Heft those trunks, bush guides,
I forgot my mirror and am keen to retrieve it
so that I may kiss my image as one would Cerberus,
if he were female
and as pretty as me.

"Emeline By Evening"

Emeline
is slender
like the chances
of crepes
in the morning.

Emeline's
skin is smooth
like sectioned glass
in the open,
black-framed
window.

Lazy traffic
glides past below;
potted geraniums
and changing lights
are red.

Try Emeline's
bed of brass and white;
her hair is short
and she calls her cat
Amante.

"A Year In The Factory"

There are thighs and then there are thighs--
yours put foreign powers on DefCon 5
out of pure jealousy.

Night shift at the factory is enough to melt skulls,
reverse the flow of hearts, turn bones to industrial byproduct
out of sheer boredom.
I loved you wearing jeans and safety goggles,
better than gown and pearls any day.

We took a picnic lunch to the city park,
and set our eyes to floating on the gray waters of the
flammable, compromised river that cuts through it.
"This is fun," we lied,
and fed bread to a one-eyed pigeon
who kept missing with his first peck.

The customs agents had stopped me the time before;
they searched my emphysemic, cookie-cutter piece of shit
right down to the wheel wells.
Holding up my rubber boots, one of them asked,
"Do you work at the plant?"
Well, what do you think, asshole? What do you think?
So you got even with them for me the next time--
you, fluent in Russian, Romanian and doubletalk
pretended not to understand the agent's fractured schoolroom parlance,
and mumbled until he let you through just to be rid of you.

How crazy that you should be Catholic--
I've never seen a craftier shoplifter.
Each time the grid went down, I kissed you for your pilfered candles,
your flashlight, your shitty little radio that kept us informed
as I buried my face in your sweetness like a supplicant.

There are thighs and then there are thighs,
and yours are the finest ever to grace my cracker box apartment
that I had to be on a waiting list for years, to get.
Everything is always in short supply--
once, you backed me through a rope of yellow hazard tape

and right into a defective forklift
with a kiss, on work time.
My shoe soles picked up God knows what from the filthy floor,
but my heart was happy
as the assembly lines rattled behind us.

There is plenty everywhere that can poison a person,
or sow cancer seeds that will explode later on.
We gave that year of our lives to the production of jugs of kitchen cleanser,
since banned.
Everyone who worked there had red hands and brittle nails,
despite the gloves, despite the icons some of us prayed to.
Oh well.
I was happy,
and even though you left just as it all seemed so good,
that year was pure, flawless, redeeming even,
like love can be sometimes,
and as your thighs definitely were, and still are,
in some other woman's bed
in another town,
where you mumble into her ear in Romanian
and she holds you closer
for all the good such motions ever do.

"coneflowers"

i left my leather boots
in the closet like buddhas,
and wore white heels to sally's summer wedding.
in the morning,
one lay in the wet grass,
and the other in the deep green leaves of the coneflower plants
at the foot of your wooden steps.

"Lies"

I was the first girl baseball star.

Babe Ruth once came to me in the holy wooden clubhouse where I dressed alone;

He arrived sober, quiet, hat in hand,

To ask my advice.

I told him:

Live temperately.

Recognize the hand of the divine in everything that you do.

Realize that the pitcher is a major leaguer, just as you are.

Be patient, wait for your pitch, but when it comes,

Swing hard and wail the living snot out of it.

I once met Mister Eddie Rickenbacker,

The celebrated flying ace.

I asked him what it was like.

He told me:

"The sky is filled with devils and blackbirds.

I find the enemy, then send them bullets like children's prayers;

When smoke begins to pour out of their machines like hubris,

They go down singing Lutheran hymns

And German beer drinking songs--

Gemini / Scorpio / Capricorn

They fall

As softly as spring rain.

I once loved a dancer

Who worked at the One Eyed Cat in Baltimore, Maryland.

She told me she had once danced

For Mister Edgar Allan Poe

On the last night of his life.

People said it was drugs,

Drink,

Bad living,

But I think he was driven mad by love for someone he could never touch.

He died scratching poetry

Into the cobblestones

With his fingernails.

I was the first girl baseball star.

I once struck out Babe Ruth.

That was when I learned

That failure can be more beautiful, sometimes, than success--

And so I went home to the gypsy camp I came from.

I told them how I'd gripped the ball

And done everything the way I'd planned to;

These women who had known me all of my life,

Just laughed toothlessly, silently,

And sent me to collect the spirit of Edgar Allan Poe.

I took him up tenderly, like an angel, or a new mother,

Stroking his filthy hair;

I told him how every time my bat kissed the ball,

It would fly far and fast into the sky, disappearing like joy over the tin Coca-Cola signs

And into the hands of some grinning urchin in a newsboy cap--

Then I kissed him

And his spirit flew away like an oriole,

Set free by my love

And gone.

"northbound / southbound"

early, i took the northbound bus,
and the whole world seemed quiet, holy and fine...
late, i took the southbound bus,
and i never saw such a devil-cursed line.

"The Succubus Athena"

When I was young, and the world too loud
Too bright
My defenses thin as tissue paper
Ridden with nightmares
Blessed with visions
Hammered with practicalities
Shoved in a box,
Unfurling only in secret
After dark
Under covers like dense fog, and I the ground,

She came.

Her owl twisted its head, as if hanged and broken-necked in a gale.
She turned hers, the picture of grace and calm.
I closed my eyes, hard.
She touched me with her black glove smooth upon my face,
And my bones gathered and rose as one,
A white flock within my flesh
A firework
A soul released and rising.

"Little girl," she said in her perfect blackwinged voice,
"What has been happening here?"
Spirits seemed to peer from behind her shoulders, listening.
A blackberry bush scraped the window outside.
The door turned its own lock and breathed.

I had believed, always, that I was dust on a smooth tabletop,
A smear,
A trial sent by someone I couldn't remember,
To perform some evil that I didn't understand.
I tried to stay out of the way.
I swallowed my words.
I was the only red spark in a house of heavy dark emplacements,
A male preserve.
I set myself on fire constantly,
In shame
In silence
Sitting politely,
Going up.

I opened my eyes.
"Who are you?" I asked the woman, my visitor.
Her owl swiveled back, to stare.
The lady's eyes widened, just for a moment,
Then narrowed.
Trees sighed, swaying above the house like mourners, unseen.
Anger floated off her, like bright dead leaves, then scattered.

She looked away.

"This must be paid for," she whispered, to the dark room.
Turning back, she was calm as a frozen sky.
She leant forward, soft as a rumor.
"I am the Succubus Athena."
"And who am I?" I asked, not even realizing it or meaning to,
And half afraid I was about to die.
For the first time, she smiled--
Dark--
Beautiful--
Perfect.
Smooth as skinning a kill, she peeled off her gloves and took my face in her hands;
She kissed my hairline, soft as the falling of full dark,
In the spot where the silver still stays.
"Little girl," she murmured, in a tone I had never heard before,
"You have always been
And will always be
Mine."

"stones"

i said i wasn't gonna throw no more stones at your window,
and mama say, if you gonna open you mouth,
tell the truth, girl, or hush.

i said i wasn't gonna throw no more stones at your window,
oh, but honey,
there were so many stones
and i missed you so much.

Gemini / Scorpio / Capricorn

"Keeping Tigers"

My tigers become restless, locked up in the house all day.
I have a service, which comes by and feeds them,
leaving carcasses
and the long bones of domestic cattle.

These meals are cold from the refrigerated truck,
and they do not struggle,
and so are not satisfying to my tigers.

I can feel their rage vibrating against the chambers of my heart as I work,
like a murmur,
or an embolism.

My tigers dream of high grasses,
dizzy with unending heat.
The sun teases them from the high windows,
until they are crazy with frustration.

The houses on my street are new, and identical.
Differentiation only arrives with occupancy--
the houses are like virgin lungs, and the buyers, air.

There is a woman inside the walls of the house across from me and over one.
The sun-hot bricks contain her, and her soft skin.
Whatever bounty she possesses
is closed off from me, as by a hard cupboard door.

I long to deliver myself into her life.
She sometimes comes out, Queen of the Green Lawn,
and when she does,
my tigers and I tear each other bloody for a place at the window.

Not everyone can keep tigers.
The daughter of the couple next door kept a bird,
a beautiful tropical specimen, which flitted from sill to ceiling fixture
to the trees outside, in summer.

When the bird disappeared, the girl reached her china-fine hand into the empty cage,
and slammed the metal door on herself

until she was bleeding so badly that paramedics had to be called.

"Were you trying to hurt yourself?" inquired the doctor.
"What made you do this?"
The girl replied, "Lack of music."

I know this because I transcribe the doctor's session recordings.
I know this because it was my tigers who murdered her bird.
I know that my silence is vile,
and that Beauty should never lower its guard around Appetite.

I grow restless in my cubicle, doing my work.
I dream of my across-the-street neighbor, and in these dreams
I run my fingertips down the backs of her thighs--
I kiss her hip, and turn her over
like a page of religious text, and I the ecstatic ecclesiastic.

In the evenings, I go home alone.
My tigers are waiting, ravenous and angry.
At my front door, I kiss the key,
and make the sign of the cross over the lock.

All night,
my tigers scratch to get into the room where I sleep.
The door quivers and splits, but holds, barely.

My neighbor is inside her house, mixing calm with catkins,
like batter with a finger.
I start across the street, though it is past midnight.

I wear only my black kimono.
My tigers trail after me, lit like candles with excitement at being out of doors.
I knock, haloed in the porch light.
She answers, and I stand there like a little innocent bird,
offering her my heart like an Aztec.

"Carmencarrion"

Darling, don't be scornful of the little cripple
selling newspapers with your headline.

It was she who taught your mother a silence so deep
that it ran through her like black blood, carrying rot;
it was the endless shushing at mama's knee
that made a dancer of you after all.

Poison, though trembling in a perfect sphere
at the tip of the world's most beautiful finger,
is still poison;
taint is still taint,
even if you christen it with a fine swung champagne
and send it down the skids into a clear blue channel.

Your fans, they love you erratic, charmingly gut-shot.
They place the rose in your teeth, and you live off the thorns.

That doctor you keep leashed at your feet
can't even find the lesions beneath the lace;
he delivers his diagnosis while dancing on his hind legs,
in traffic,
with silly paper hearts taped over his eyes.

In the end, you still manage to remain obscure
even while performing, spot lit, in front of thousands.
You are a snappish, self-governing state
draped in silk, and wearing a stylish hat groaning with feathers.

Darling, don't be scornful of the little cripple.
Don't do her your turned brand of vile mischief,
then walk away in three inch heels,
laughing.

Your reviews have been slipping, and your notices turn up in birds' nests
with the dead mice and blank-eyed fledglings.

Feel the clips in your hair, like talons.
Sense your mother's eyes on you from out in the red plush seats,
though the footlights stop you from locating the bleed.

Take my hand.
Trust me.
I'll lead, just this once, light as a draught horse,
and you, Darling,
why, you will follow down stage
like a pretty hearse,
driverless and sinking
through the brittle ice and into obscurity.

"Love Poem In Extremis"

Go down by the graveyard, darling;
I'll be there,
Carrying my patent leather heels in my hand.

Meet me where the headstones lean.
Wear a veil.
Come out of a cloud of crows, like a black sun.

My feelings for you stun me, always.
I am gripped with heart attack.
I fight for breath.

I wore a hussy's black lace for you,
And lied like a viper about where I was going;
Look around, everyone is dead. There is no one to sniff and deplore.

I am on my back in the decaying leaves,
Beneath a weeping angel made of stone.
Come to me, I beg you.

Under lowering clouds in late-day dusk,
Let's fuck as if our lives depend upon it--
Because they do, sweetheart,
They do.

"The Dime Priest"

I sat with the dime priest on the steps of Saint T's, like a paper cup blown up against a holy statue in a garden.

I said,

"I am falling, falling. I am an ice chunk;

My mother the sky has farmed me out to her sister the earth,

Via express delivery."

The dime priest looks over, his huge hands dangling over his knees as if waiting for some greater work.

"What's wrong, Pookie?" he asks me simply, tilting his chin up.

He could have starred in movies.

"The tense has changed," I point out irrelevantly.

"It always does," he tells me with a shrug.

We watch the traffic in front of us, and the clouds above. No stop lights there. No brakes, either.

I love the dime priest. He is so queer and kind.

"Maybe I should say confession."

He looks down and laughs, his broad shoulders shaking.

"I may as well take it from a cat. You don't know what 'no' is, except for just an obstacle,

Something placed out of reach

Just to vex you."

Why can't I marry the dime priest?

I would make sure his vestments were always clean and mended.

He would make sure never to let me fall into the deep end of my heart.

We would fix our favorite coffee;

Always defend each other to strangers,

Never have sex,

And be smiled upon by some god somewhere,

Wouldn't we?

I am a spill, spreading.

He is the quicker picker upper.

"Who is she, Pookie?"

I falter, like a papier-mache bird caught in the rain.

"She is out of reach, like God.

She is funny and crazy, like the commandments.

She rides inside of something else, like Jonah.

Her faith wavers, like the heat over a fire.

She's just some woman I met," I add miserably.

He will look over at me, with those matinee idol eyes

And I will see that he's on to me,

Like everybody's on to me--

And he will know that I love this one,

Just like everybody knows I do--

And I will fall apart on the steps of Saint T's, and he will pat me with his bear paws and say,

"Aw, Pookie, it's gonna be okay."

I will say, into his black shirt, "The tense has changed again."

He will say, "It always does,"

And then he will be

The dollar priest

And I will be

Scattered change.

"Canto For A Cuckoo"

Once upon a springtime came
A pretty bird made of flame;
I opened both my heart and nest
I loved its song, I loved its breast--

It stayed a while and lit up May;
It warmed my heart, I bade it stay.
I loved it well, I loved it best--

But when the flame bird goes,
The ashes blow
From east to west--

That's the rest.

"God & Eros"

As a child, I was given a skull and a knife to play with.

I turned the skull on its back, so it could look up and see God.
I gave it the knife for an eye, to sharpen its vision.

I said, "Dollie, what do you see?"
She said, "One eye sees a silver blade,
the other sees a table of sky."

For a long time, we played God and Girl,
my knife-eyed Dollie and me.
She said, "The clouds are plates,
the birds are tea cups."

I said, "Here are my fingers for spoons,
and a sugar of bones for our bowl."

My mother was angry that year.
She blew through like sleet.

"What are you doing?" she demanded,
cleverly using the Wind's voice to accuse.
"Playing church," I lied.

When I grew up, I used knife eyed Dollie's face to make some Woman love me.
"You see so much," she said.

I am the restless wolf with the moon in its mouth.
I make crows crazy with their own very blackness.

"Good girl," said the Woman,
And I kissed her hard.

"Admission"

You asked me for a song,
My googly-eyed little lamblet;
In the dying hours of a dying day,
You asked me for life, for music,
For some bright trifle to stay despair.

Could I be mother to all of that?
Fuckinay, Bo Peep,
To all of that and more.

I give you credit.
You didn't resort to the old roundhouse
And try to beat it out of me
As so many have before,
Pressing "sorry" to my bruises like a beefsteak
While promising never, ever, to do it again.

They were Catholics, my lovers,
All in an access of crossing themselves,
Particularly their fingers
Behind their suspendered backs--
And that was the women.

So, a tune you wish,
A tune you shall have.
Let me rosin my bow with the ground bones of Pharaohs.
This wood comes from Italy;
My remarkable fingers from my Gypsy aunts.
My skirts are Parisian,
And my smile that you love so well?
That came from seven devils, dead lo these seven years.

Sit.
You may use my lavender-colored fainting couch.
Recline, like a lime in gin.
Drape my burnt rose scarf over the Tiffany lamp.
Close your eyes.

You asked me for a song,
In the dying hours of a dying day;

For life, for music,
For some bright trifle to stay despair--
Let it be my love, for I do love you,
Despite my gloomy black gloves
And the way I flinch, like a tethered bird,
With every honest note I dare to play.

"Kids"

We were just kids.

We liked Patti Smith, Pat Benatar and Quarterflash.

We drank a lot of wine and bowling alley gin.

The law was 18.

We were going no place, in thrift store leather jackets.

We read French poets, and didn't understand a word.

We had no plans,

But we had each other.

It was grand and glorious and stupid and temporary.

We were as random as a sack of cats.

We thought we were smart;

We were not always wrong.

We were nobody, but we were us.

We were just kids.

"Love Poem For K."

My house is small.
If I buy an orange,
And bring it home in a canvas bag,

I have to decide what to get rid of;
What object it will replace.

If I lose something--
My book of Whitman poems, or
The card from my friend in New York,

It's bound to be right there,
As close as coffee to the cup.

Should the postman drop me a letter,
I must then send one out.
I dream only once each night, but richly.

There would seem to be no room
For Another
In my life,

And yet,
The sun comes through my window
Each morning,

And seems to belong there.
What about that?

"Pantry Chef"

When I was younger,
I washed lettuce heads in cold water.
I would set them on my cutting board, gently,
As if my hands hummed with lullabies.

I lifted tomatoes from their cardboard carton beds.
I lined them in a row like nursery babies,
And my starched jacket was always white and clean.

I knew romaine and bibb,
Beefsteak and cherry.
I kept my hair tied back, my nails short,
The right knife sharp and at the ready.

I didn't know, then
That lovers remember the wine, not the greens;
The sugar, not the side plate.

I wish you were here to kiss my hands
With their swollen knuckles and cut-scars.
What was I doing with my tenderness
When I had someone who wanted it?

When I was younger,
I had a paying job, a small talent,
And a driver with a dolly at the back door
Coming every day to keep my walk-in cooler stocked.

I thought that was bounty.
I thought there was no harm in staying on through another fall.
I never considered that what I made was not mine,
Or that someone else was paying for it all.

Gemini / Scorpio / Capricorn

"My Sixth Life"

I brought her early light in a leather pouch,
And a snake's head in a handkerchief.
What a fool I was.

Every April, she crouched on the muddy roads
Like something not human.
First warmth carries taint,
And she rolled until she was filthy with it;
Don't think there weren't those who admired her.

A sick sky will deny that it ever held clouds
And a thousand lies without pause will make it rain,
If only in the upturned palm of a lunatic.

I brought her a ring made from poisonous metal,
And instructions on how to drown herself.
A gray cat is no haloed nun,
So if I grew claws from the ends of my fingers,
It was only to prove before the maypoles went up
That God was mad or that she was.

"god"

god sees when you do bad, mama said.
does not, i said.
does. god sees everything.
this was bad news and i didn't care for it.

then i don't like god, i said.
i'll give god a bloody nose.
can't, said mama.
your arms are too short.

jenny at school say
it's against the rules.
jenny say
i'm gonna tell.
but jenny ain't god.
guess how i know?

Shay Caroline Simmons, Kelli Simpson, Joy Ann Jones

"The Boring Lover"

(dedicated to the detectives of the major case squad.)

Madeleine's lover becomes boring--
She longs to simply push him off the balcony,
And watch him fall like an old cherished hope.

Once,
Madeleine felt as close to him
As the pomade on his hair.
Constantly, she whispered in his ear
Words of devotion as sweet as any lozenge.

But now,
Though she searches her heart as if it were The Golden Shoulder Bag,
She has to admit that he has become work-a-day,
And no different, really,
From any other man;
He has become the proverbial
Ordinary Brand.

When she suggests that they go dancing,
He looks slightly shocked
As if she had proposed that they drown the cat,
Or go downstairs together to seduce the doorman.
Sometimes she spreads his good tuxedo out on the bed
And lays her head on it, silently.

Madeleine knows
That Death could free her from him--
That if he had to clutch something in the last instant,
It would be his tiresome drug store cigar and not her hand.
Not even the pitiless pavement below
Could make him give it up.

Madeleine imagines
That if she pushed her dull lover off the balcony,
A detective would arrive and step out of the elevator as if he were a vended soda.
He would come in and sit in the chintz chair.
He would ask, "Why did you kill?"
"He smoked," she would reply.

The detective would set down his tea cup,
Put away his pen,
And say, "I know that these things happen.
I know you are a good person."
Then he would add, kindly,
"I know a nice little place where they play a mean rhumba.
Would you like to go?"
And she would say,
"Handsome,
I thought you'd never ask."

"Everybody Loves The Sun"

(for K.)

Everybody loves the sun.
You live your life in it, wear it like honeyskin,
But it is your darkness I have always adored.

I will wait
Until your life lets you go, to me,
In the interstice between clock beats--
Baby, I have
One boot heel on the ground,
And the other up against the wall;
All of me is in shadow...
The gates here are beautiful but hard.

You'll come, won't you?
I am your girl with the astigmatic soul,
Waiting, depending upon tactile sense and white witchcraft;
I am the Other One, who nests your name.
Everybody loves the sun,
But I love only you.

Shay Caroline Simmons, Kelli Simpson, Joy Ann Jones

"Strippers"

A pole dancer and a minister move in together.

They don't love each other, but,

They agree that everyone else is an asshole.

They are both sick of the needy looking to them for what they cannot find at home.

They hand out titillation, or cans from the food bank, with the same smile, and the same withering scorn.

Their friends are all horrified.

"How can you move in with someone like that?" they ask, eyes wide.

But in the night, she asks him to recite scripture to her. His chest is hairy, it's like passing out on someone's front porch with her face on the bristly doormat.

The words he says are loony gibberish, but his voice is like newspaper trucks rumbling by in the pre-dawn; his arms are a porch light and she the moth.

In the night, he touches his fingertips to her skin, and finds that she is smoother than a surplice. It is like being handed the bowl, for the sweet batter within.

He knows her history, the cafeteria line of her past lovers hovering like moondogs, but in her arms he feels that she is braille, and he the blind man.

People begin to notice changes.

She quits the club and takes up dancing at her kitchen sink.

He quits the ministry and finds himself suddenly mute, but his hearing improves.

Their friends are horrified.

"You've changed. I knew this would happen!" they say, eyes wide.

The pole dancer and the minister move away.

They live in a dinky place, but

They love each other.

Their neighbors smile, but regard them with withering scorn.

They think the couple are bohemians, and if there's a cat left in the local shelter, it must be because those two missed it.

She likes the cats for their physical grace.

He likes them for their silence.

Neither of them goes to clubs, or to church.

They make new friends.

The friends say, "One day at a time, keep coming back," and other loony gibberish.

The sun comes up, the sun goes down.

If they keep living on the Mobius Strip,

They may just find themselves yet.

"Done, Devil"

What have you done, Devil?
Jimmying the front door this time was a cute touch.
Look at my walls, my rugs--
What have you done, Devil?
I suppose you're going to clean this up?

Devil, get behind me.
Rhumba down,
Cha cha back.
Look at all the black heel marks on my precious linoleum--
Look at all your stolen souls, gone amok.
Who is going to control them?

Devil, let me straighten your tie.
If I didn't know better, I might think that you had arrived
A tiny bit high.
Have a cupcake, Devil.
I made them myself, and went to no small trouble.
Of course they're chocolate!
You're such a fuckwit.

Devil, you think you're so wickedly smart--
You smear brimstone on the hearth stone
And tell me it's pop art.
Be glib--
Very nice, very well.
Let me say this in the most loving way:
You don't look so good.
You've let yourself go all to hell.

Til next time, Devil.
Go walk up and down upon the Earth.
Do whatever it is you do,
But for what it's worth,
Pink is the new red, and goes just as nice with classic black.
Oh, don't try to tell me, Devil,
That you never thought of that.

"A Serengeti Gospel"

I was called by the matrilineal.

Already, from my grandmother, I had learned that one who lies so still will not rise again except in dreams;

From my aunt, I learned that laughter vexes the devil. Her example came loudly and often, delighting the child that I was;

And from my mother I learned that nothing is safe, and not to trust love.

I wanted more. I longed to join the lionesses, and so I sold my car, my house, my jewelry,

And found myself at the edge of the Serengeti.

I stripped down and walked into the heart of lion country.

You may think,

This was a fool's errand;

But the lionesses recognized me at once, and immediately I found myself

Watching the cubs,

Joining the hunt.

My body grew brown and tough,

My nails long and sturdy.

I crouched in the tall grasses with the others, and as we stalked the buffalo herd,

I looked at my sisters and their avid teeth, their golden eyes shining and I recalled a woman,

In an upstairs flat in summer time.

She called me "you sweet sweet bitch." That was the first time.

Then we are bursting into the open in streaks of yellow,

Like shooting stars,

And I am where I belong.

We are the lionesses, and we stay together for life.

The males come and go, depending upon who beats the daylights out of who at any given time.

That is not my concern.

My concern is to kill.

There is no cruelty in it, only pragmatic necessity.

If I return with nothing, my children cannot eat mercy.

For them, it is dinner or death, and so I chase, spring, and strike,

Without remorse;

And after all, I did not invent this arrangement.

This night, I have run to ground a member of a television reality program;

As I crush my victim's throat, a man wearing a baseball cap cries, "Are you getting this? Are you getting it?!?"

I drag the dead actor away.

Hyenas harass me, but my sisters come to my aid and we leave one of the thieves with an opened flank.

We eat well, growing lazy and contented.

This has become my home.

My life is bound together with the others;

I have almost forgotten that I am human,

And this is not such a bad thing.

A camera woman using night vision trains her lens on me--

I feel something,

Something,

Then I dip my head and show my teeth.

Whatever it was is gone.

"My Hands At Night"

(for K.)

My hands were dreaming--
One, of the warm skin just below your left breast...
Of your ribs as you breathe, and the beauty of your heart beat.

The other, of your hair in fingerfuls,
A soft rope ladder to summer night rain before it falls.

I set my hands outside, in the grass, without waking them.
There were fireflies
And endless stars.

"Beeville"

Beeville is the kind of place you move away from.

There are silos and an IGA out on Miller Road, out by the old assembly plant.

Its heavy chains loop around the gates like yarn in a girl's hair,

But of course,

Girls haven't worn yarn in their hair for decades.

Out at Beeville High,

The boys' football team is practicing--

They are called the Bucks

And bucked is what they are.

Ricky Lundquist is the best they can do;

The kids call him Fat Ricky

And the football squibs out of his fingers like a link sausage from the hand of an infant

Playing with its food at the IHOP down Highway 90.

The last time Beeville won anything,

It was the lady Bucks in 1990.

They rode their ancient bus to Chesaning and Fowlerburg,

And Becky MacGruder's hook shot would arc through the gyms like a bright planet in the winter sky.

She kicked ass,

Gemini / Scorpio / Capricorn

And all the lady Bucks would hit the DQ on the way back,

The yellow bus bouncing over the pot holes in the lot

Like a happy drunken duck.

Becky MacGruder has kids of her own now.

They wear a lot of crap around their wrists and necks

And howl like the damned if made to stay home on a Saturday night.

Sometimes if the doorbell rings or the dog gets into something,

Becky will shift her laundry basket from a hip to the stairs

And go off down the hall just like she was driving the lane.

When she gets back,

With somebody's sweatshirt in her hand, plucked off the back of the couch or a kitchen chair,

She balls it up

And sinks it in the laundry basket from fifteen feet,

Nothing but plastic.

Beeville lady Bucks!

Yeah!

It's still on the sign out on Miller Road, even though the "a" in "ch mpions" has fallen off.

They locked up the title

On a crisp night in March--

Locked it up tight like the gates of the assembly plant,

And even Mr. MacGruder, who hardly ever said two words in a week,

Told his daughter how very proud of her he was.

"Mission"

On a dead planet with nine moons
I said,
This cannot stand.
This will never do.
He said,
Is it the constant storms?
Is it the greenless wastes where nothing ever grew?
I said no dear,
Not that, dear...
It's you.

Nine moons around my head
Nine pentagrams around my bed
Can't watch or pray
The devil away
Because,
Because,
I keep her close and my hatred fed.

The lightning flashes and strikes at last
And all this sand is turned to glass--
It cuts me
And splits me
Now I think
It may be

That there are ten of me
Or ten thousand,
Ten million,
And each with its own little coal black heart--
Never to forgive you.
Never to part.

Gemini / Scorpio / Capricorn

"House Of Wax"

He moved her into a house filled with spirits,

Then brought in that gloomy, ring-eyed excorcist

Before she'd had the chance to sleep with half of them.

No wonder he fell down the basement stairs

Christmas Eve,

His egg nog balanced perfectly unspilled on the second step,

Him at the bottom,

Staring broken-necked at the dryer.

These things happen, said the firemen,

Snapping their gurney open smartly and removing him on it too soon,

Before she'd had the chance to sleep with half of them.

No wonder their alarms keep going off

At exactly midnight in the firehouse

When there is no emergency

And the telephones make that awful off-the-hook whining noise

Inside their heads.

All I'm trying to say,

Is if you come to stay,

Kiss her softly,

Welcome her crossed ankles across your back,

And remember--

There's plenty of time to fill your lungs in the sunrise,

Hours from now,

Haunted and scented like last night's candle,

Rolled out the back door

And into the light.

"She"

she
got a wild-ass dog that sleeps with her.
she
swears a blue streak.
she
don't speak no yankee.
she
rather drive than fly.
she
rocks a sweet pair of boots.
she
don't listen to no shit music.
she
the only one in the room, to me.
she.

"Saint Creola"

St. Creola keeps canaries
and doesn't care if they crap on the
good
back-snapping
for-show
furniture
that's been rolled in here like coffins at a starting line.

St. Creola keeps cats
and that, dear little pie-eyed pilgrim,
keeps the birds from getting sedentary
or old.
Behold,
another miracle of the beautiful St. Creola.

So,
has rain afflicted your world until
great monsters leap from the guttering?
Does the devil
sleep with your girlfriend,
help herself to your make-up,
your feather bed,
and your little funky vintage Renault?

Tell St. Creola,
like she could care,
like the jelly buttered muffin would stop at her mouth
and she would say, her eyes filling with blessed tears,
oh,
angel...

Pffft,
sweet canary,
land here,
learn.
Today St. Creola has called the moving men,
so muscular that they ripple while standing still.
They will roll the coffins off the cliff at San Creola,
birthplace of Our Lady;
Honey, she will live forever,
as will her parasol,

as will all who love her,
cleansed in the spray of the coffins returning like swallows to the sea.

St. Creola is serene.
She offers her hand--
kiss it!
Tonight you will share her bed, and in the morning
sleep right through services.
Let your softness leave her boneless, beatific, even a little bruised;
certainly in no condition to notice how
when you pray now,
your gaze is always up
where the birds chirp and flutter
like excited virgins.

"Crow In Love"

A crow flew
Three feathers fell
One to the wind
One to the earth
And one straight down into hell

The trees turned to ice
Then into sand
The crow couldn't look
The crow couldn't breathe
The crow couldn't find where to land

This is the country of love, said the other birds
Make three chicks from the feathers that fall
One heart of ice
One heart of sand
And your favorite, with no heart at all

A crow flew
Her loneliness turned her black
Her wings turned to stone
So she couldn't fly on
And god knows, she couldn't go back.

"Decompensation"

I had a fever, but only in one eye.

I opened it--

Tripped-out fractals,

Colors,

Bullshit.

I closed it--

My naked love

With a wicked smile on her gone-gypsy face.

I wrote poems, but only with one hand.

The other did the most batshit-crazy things, all unbidden--

Got a job,

Wore a ring,

Spooned pablum til I wanted to cut it off and fling it away.

So I cut it off and flung it away.

Now I spend afternoons reading Soap Opera Digest by the freeway,

Nestled between two stone-loony lunging German Shepherds I have named Bonnie and Clyde

But I call them

Doll-Baby and Pookie-Face,

And I wink at them as I feed them Sonic burgers and stroke them with my stump.

They know

That I have a beautiful heart,

And who but them will love this heart?

I have a fever, but only in one eye.

I open it--

Tripped-out fractals,

Colors,

Bullshit.

I close it--

My naked love

With a wicked smile on her gone-gypsy face.

"December 23rd"

It was two days before Christmas,
And I hadn't seen the riders in the road.
I remember
The big bay doing a stutter step,
His head moving down, then up,
Like an oil well.

I swerved my car into the trees
As if I were a child down a slide--
Whump! Fast.
Into a parent's arms.

"Sit here," someone said.
Kindly,
A request.
I knew I was dead.
It was snowing outside--
Big exuberant flakes, coming down
In the halo of the porch light beyond the windows...
I hadn't expected that.

Soft sounds came from inside the kitchen doorway.
A hall clock ticked,
Comfortingly.
I studied the dark richness of the old plank floor,
And soaked in the soothing gray
Of the walls.

Then,
A woman came and leaned in the light near the stairway.
"Hi," she said, and smiled.
She wore a ribbed turtleneck and jeans,
With antique silver rings on her fingers,
And her blond hair was the color of honey on biscuits.

"I'm dead," I told her, stupidly.
"I know," she said, and held out her hand. "Are you ready?"
"Sure," I heard myself say,
And I was.

---

2. Poems by Kelli Simpson

"Dog Days"

I spend hours
roaming the stubbled hayfields,
catching grasshoppers,
and feeding them to the cats.
I've been told that eating too many will burn them up inside,
but I don't believe it.
The cats don't seem to believe it, either.

It's so hot you can hear it.

There's always a cool spot
in the mud at the edge of the pond,
but you have to crawl under
the willow tree to get there.
I go in slow and watch for water moccasins
curled in the branches above.

I've faced more fearsome monsters.

Sunset spreads like a bruise
across the sky.
The tin roof of the barn,
still warm to the touch,
bears my weight and holds my secrets.
I'm the highest point in the emptiness.

And, the stillness is so vast that I don't make a ripple.

"Skin"

When the sun rides high
through the longest days,
it calls my native blood
and I darken like a berry.
My hips sway like bluestem.
I call the moon by its name.

Out on the porch swing,
my head in your lap,
your fingers toy with my bear grease braid,
and I whisper stories
that would make even your God weep.
You nod, but there is no knowing,
so I fall silent
and let your cool, white hands
study history
in the warmth of my blood-bronze skin.

"Hourglass"

The sand in the hourglass
seems sluggish
so I give it a quick shake,
as if time will respond to rough treatment
and bring you back to me
faster.

"Witching Water"

Witching water is lonely work.
Joined to the rod and the red dirt,
there is little time for children
or a constant man.
But, I have crumpled bills in my pocket,
a swallow of whiskey left in the bottle,
and a feathered branch that never lies
when it turns in my hand
and cries "water!"

"The River"

When you asked if I could swim,
I tried to pull back from the river.

When they asked you how I drowned and died,
you wept, a broken man.

The preacher said what God has joined
let no man put asunder,

so God must have let you push me under
with your cheating hands.

Yet, here I am,
penning verse
from the comfort of my funeral hearse.
The devil must not be done with me yet.

He sucked the water from my lungs
and sucked The Word right off my tongue,
and I think it's only fair I pay my debt

and feed the river.

"The Nest"

I hollowed my bones
so I could fly
never thinking how fragile I'd become.

I hollowed my heart
so your good-bye
had a comfortable place to rest.

I pieced a quilt from hollow words
to chase the chill of loneliness,
but the hollow of your shoulder warms me best.

Like a bird fallen from the nest,
I just want to go home.

"Poet/Mother"

Beach pail seeds took root

What's that kid doing in the street?

and grew into sand castles

Is that your kid in the street?

that swallowed the sea.

Hey, kid! Get out of the street!

"Snakes"

We twine together like snakes,
skin sliding against skin,
breathless in our sacred space.

You are birth and death and chocolate,
pulling pins from my hair until curls fall
like second thoughts.

Painting my lips with sweetness
until I taste
and realize how long I've been hungry.

"Mail"

The spider walks my back,
stringing silk with every step.
The promise of rain
dries my mouth
and wets me inside.

I've been parched as prairie grass
since your last letter.
I've read it,
held it,
wrung the sweetness out of every word,
and now nothing remains
but cloudless paper
and famished ink.
Its brittle edges leave dust
upon my tongue.

Mine has been a raven's vigil.
But, now, thunder beats like a heart on the horizon.
The webs hang empty in the corners.
And, the spider sleeps at the nape of my neck.

Have you written, my love?
It smells like rain.

"Moon Water"

Water spills from the moon's open hand.
From where I stand
on the sandy shore,
I can see the droplets meet the lake
and make ripples
lasting longer than you ever loved me.

"Had"

Kiss me
and let my red arsenic lips
mark you mine.

Touch me
and let my body surround you
like an echo.

Take me
and know
that you've been had.

"Modern Bride"

Zombie brides prefer chiffon
and carry lilies made of ash.
Zombie brides tend not to last long.
Zombie brides aren't much for love songs.

Zombie grooms sport tattered tails
and bear a ring still on the knuckle.
Zombie grooms wear mismatched socks
and carry livers in a box

just in case one of the guests requires a spare.

"A Lot Going On"

You're a parade -
marching bands,
batons glinting in the sun,
candy tossed in the street.

You're a stampede -
hooves thudding
like my heart
every time you're near.

You're a road trip -
without a map,
taking me where I didn't know
I wanted to go.

You're a lot going on
for one woman,
don't you know?

"Sway"

If you lift my hair
and let the night air whisper
kisses on my neck,
my throat, my moon bare shoulder,
I will sway like a willow.

"Pretzel"

I drop into the next pose
with the grace of a drunken elephant,
all awkward arms
and uncooperative legs.

My sweaty hair has escaped its confines
and hangs in my face.
Out of the corner of my eye,
I can see
the swinging to and fro of a wayward barrette.

My panties are creeping toward my ovaries.

"Breathe," intones the perfectly coiffed, panty line-less instructor. "Don't forget to breathe."

So, I exhale
a serene and silent chorus . . .

fuck you fuck you fuck you.

"Waiting"

Come to me, my love.
I am tangled and tender,
blushing and breathless,
sweet as an offering of
dark incense and spice.

"MsUnderstood"

Somewhere in the backseat
were my panties and the remains of the liquor.
I was searching for either or
when you lit a cigarette and muttered,
"I have a bed, you know."

It was then that I knew that you expected to be relevant.

With a disappointed sigh
I realized
that no matter how many times
I gave it up
you were never gonna get me.

When I dance naked in the headlights,
you blame the whiskey.

When I drive you mad with my mouth
and laugh
because I can,
you see a lover's eyes.

You can't see the liar for the lies.

You're just watching smoke
while the fire goes untended
and flickers out
beneath a gravedigger's moon.

"Kiss The Cook"

Sugar on my fingertips
and slowly drifting to the floor.
Suck the sugar from my lips.

Flour hand prints on my hips
on the walls, on the floor.
Sugar on my fingertips.

A dash of that, a pinch of this
melt, measure, knead, pour.
Suck the sugar from my lips.

Turn up the heat and gently mix
melt, measure, need more.
Sugar on my fingertips.

All the flavors we adore
and, some we've never tried before.
Sugar on my fingertips.
Suck the sugar from my lips.

"Dinner Wear"

Tonight, let's dress for dinner.
I'll wear resentment like an ugly sweater.
You can slip into your favorite sense of entitlement.
We'll put on some Mahler,
throw the good china,
and kick the dog.

We can talk about the good old days
as if there were any,
or the future
as if there is one.

We can make love
as we both think of someone else.
Then, we can fall asleep in each other's arms
like two cadavers in a coffin.

"Heat"

I want to strip you
with lush and transcendent words
that leave you
lost in languor.

I want to pour you
a river of wine
that pools in the harbor of your hips.

I want to press my breasts
against your chest
until our hearts fall silent.

I want to
seduce you
in the sun.

"Shoes"

The roses that you brought this morning
smelled like dog piss
and wilted well before noon.
That, and you tracked a mess
of strange dirt all over my kitchen floor.

My horoscope said that you was a waste
of my powerful carnal energies.

But, what can I say?
I love a nice pair of shoes.

"Walk"

Lace your fingers with mine
and walk with me.
It's just a little rain.
Let's match our footsteps
and nestle in each other's silence.
I have others for the words I say.
But, I have only you
for what I leave unsaid.
Lace your fingers with mine
and walk with me a while.

"The Mind Of God"

God takes her coffee black,
no sugar.

I didn't have to ask.
I can read God's mind.

God thinks tea parties
are for children and glassy-eyed dolls.
She'll make it rain
when she damn well pleases.

I didn't have to ask.
I can read God's mind.

God has a soft spot for widows and orphans.
She sends all attempts to "pray away the gay"
directly to voice mail.
She does not own a corporate jet.

I didn't have to ask.
I can read God's mind.

Shay Caroline Simmons, Kelli Simpson, Joy Ann Jones

"Threes"

I was little more than a girl
when I started keeping company with death.
He didn't know me by name;
I was just a worker in his fields,
tending frail, palsied fruits
until the appointed times of each.

I never begrudged him his harvest.

I came to know his ways, though.
I could feel his footsteps along my spine,
catch the faintest drift of cinnamon and decay in the air,
and notice the exact moment when the birds
nesting in the north wing stairwell
hushed their song.

I know that he always takes in threes.

Six days ago, just after my first round,
he came for Mrs. Faulkner.
Hers was a quiet, pretty death.
Four days later, Mr. Layton clung to his final breath so fiercely
that I lost my usual indifference
and left work early to come home.

That's when I saw you with her.

Tell me, do you smell cinnamon?

"Store Bought Peach"

You're like a store bought peach,
all promise on the outside,
but stone beneath the skin.

I hold you in my farm girl hands,
wise to the sweet weight of ripe
and unmoved by a flawless blush;
there is no give beneath my fingers.

Like a store bought peach,
you'll never soften till you rot.

"Home"

I'm not the clay goddess that you've made.
I'm not the sacred bones that you have buried.
I'm not a tender shoot sprung from your earth.
I'm the woman that you married.

And, if your clay toys crumble,
and feral dogs find your bones,
if drought deprives the tender shoot,
you can still come home.

"Instructions"

If I go to crazy and don't make it back,
bring her up to love Jesus.
Remember that she likes her milk warm and her peas frozen.
Let her make you laugh.

If she asks, tell her
that a blue sky bird may break a wing,
but that broken bird will still sing.
Tell her to listen
in the quiet of the morning.

"Others"

There have been others.
Conveniences, really.
But, no one has undone me
with a look
the way you do,
made me ache
with a smile,
the way you do,
enveloped me
the way you do
without even trying.

"Untitled"

As I write haiku,
you read Plath and try to edge
me toward the oven.

"The Kiss"

Kiss me. Liquefy
my bones until I puddle
like spilled honey. Chase

my rolling sweetness
down and claim it with your teeth.
Breathe deep of my dark

sandalwood and smoke,
but don't choke on my embers.
Kiss me to my knees.

"Bartholomew"

You gave me your blessing
and a promise of fair weather.
I gave you head
in an empty bathroom stall.

Bartholomew

May the saints preserve us
like little jars of pickles
stacked against the cellar wall.

I chased the end of summer
playing guitar for the folkies.
You got a steady job
selling Nikes at the mall.

Bartholomew

I know you don't deserve this,
but I've met a pretty singer,
and I've promised her the fall.

We left with your blessing
and a warning about the weather
and a brand new pair of Nikes
I shoplifted from the mall.

Bartholomew

I wish you could come with us,
and if you're ever down in Katy,
promise me you'll call.

"The Novice"

I am a young witch,
new to the arts,
but already skilled in spells and alchemy.
It is waning summer
and time to gather potion plenty.

Staff in hand,
I meander rutted paths
and gather

the feather of a bird
the dust from a coyote track
the blood of an aloe

and return to my cauldron
to mix, measure,
and murmur the wind
until I am called back
by my mother's exasperated voice.

She sees mud pies and mess.
But, in the long shadows,
I am making magic.

"Lost And Found"

Lost is any place
you're not. Found is wherever
you happen to be.

"September"

September light
filters through the eaves,
and the old barn gets religion.
We are angels
with hay in our hair.

Beneath us,
boards creak and moan
songs from the back of the hymnal.
Your name
is a prayer on my lips.

I have apples
picked from the low branches.
You have your hands
high up my skirt.

Sweet is the harvest this time of year.
Sweet and tender the harvest.

"Feed"

I have patience with
you, my bride. You wax, you wane;
I'll feed when you're full.

As you work your way
through the sky. You wax, you wane;
I'll feed when you're full.

Pulling my blood like
a warm tide. You wax, you wane;
I'll feed when you're full.

I'm patient,
but I'll not be denied.

"Remember, Grasshopper…"

She who chooses where
to place the bullseye tends to
be the better shot.

"The Help"

I make excuses
and call them reasons.

I'm older and fatter.
We're busy.
You're tired.

The truth is much simpler.

No one really sees the help.

"Side Of The Road"

Loose gravel and loose
morals got me in this ditch.
A warm beer and a

little leg might get
me out, but this is nowhere.
So, I kick back on

the tailgate, wish on
an early star, and let the
pumpjack rhythm get

under my skin and
simmer. The beer I'll just keep
for my own sweet self.

"The Botanist"

Was it love
that thrust your hands
into my dirt
and sent your fingers searching
until they found
my tender roots?

Was it love
that had you lift me high
and carry me
like a prize
through my wild and tangled woods?

And, was it love
that made you give me
pride of place
in this manicured space
of choking tidiness?

If so, I don't think that I care for love.
It feels too much like dying.

"Soap"

Mama made me suck soap till I spit suds,
till I sputtered and choked and swore that I'd
never! never! say such a word
as the word she heard me say that
day when I was chasing little Eddie
away from my collection of earthworms.

But, it seems I was born with a dirty
mouth. Just as I've sworn to quit swearing, a
"Bullshit! Fuck You!" slips out, and it
feels so fine to cross the line of
proper ladylike behavior that I
(sorry, Mama) savor every word.

"Little Summer"

It was little summer,
and I'd promised you I'd come.
So, I packed my bag
and left my pride
and took the last train out of Bedlam.

When you met me at the station,
I turned the other cheek,
but your scent
(richer than remembrance)
left me breathless on my feet.

There was a ride I don't remember.
A meal I didn't taste.
Careful conversation saying nothing.

Till I said,

"Walk me up the stairs.
Pretend that I'm your wife.
Swift and sure unhook my dress
like you do it every night.
Push aside the velvet.
Claim me with your kiss.
You've promised her forever;
all I have is this.
It's little summer,
and fall is closing in."

We made love in a strange bed.
We'll never have our own.
Then I packed up what was left of me
and took the train back home.

You returned to Autumn.
Some seasons never change.
Me, I reaped our season's planting;
Little Summer is her name.

"Anything"

I can soak my tongue in sweet, sweet words
and find the tenderest parts of you.
Or, roll my tongue in salty truth
and learn to love the sting.

For you, anything.
For you, anything.

I can lie, genteel, like a lady,
or be the woman unafraid to scream.
I can burn through you hot as daylight,
or be the cool comfort darkness brings.

For you, anything.
For you, anything.

Anything at all.

"The Cloth"

Having spent a good portion
of the previous night dreaming
of riding the dark wave of your hips,
our breath mingling,
our voices joining in a rising crescendo -
"oh God, oh GOD, OH GOD"
until we splintered
like the couch beneath us,

I could not help but blush
when you placed the wafer
on my tongue.

"On Reading That Poem"

It was like being kissed.
Not the fumbling first kiss
of paragraphs and prose,
but a kiss so lyrical against my lips
that my skin sang in answer.

It was like being touched
line
by line
by line
until my breath came fast and rough.

It was like being loved.
Every phrase.
Every word.
It was like being loved.

"Plainly"

"Speak plainly, poet,"
you say with a laugh,
and my words fly
like startled birds
so I kiss you.

Once-
quickly-
before you can speak.
Twice-
deeply-
until we sink
to the ground together,

and our lips' simple couplet
says more
than a sky full of verse.

"All But One"

The old sow went mad
in the midst of her labor
and began eating her young.
It was the winter I turned eleven.

For days, the air had been thick
with flu and flurries.
Fever had baked my brain and bones
in such hallucinatory heat
that I mistook my grandmother's cries
for dregs of dreams.
Still, I pulled on my boots
and waded out into the snow.

The sow that I had raised from a piglet
lay on her side in a sheltered corner of the lot.
Her newly concave sides shuddered with every breath.
Snot and mud crusted her snout.
The sad remains of her litter bloodied the churned snow.

She had ripped them to shreds.
All but one.

"Crook Or Craft"

By crook or craft or
pale moonlight, I'll have your lips
'fore the pass of night.

And, I'll have your skin,
bloodless and bare, wrapped round my
bones; I'll have your hair.

Your skull, your spine, your
tend'rest parts. But, fear not, love,
you can keep your heart.

"Shakespeare's Fall"

You like the way
I drop my g's
when I read Shakespeare to you
in bed,

the way my r's are soft
as the side of my breast,

and the way I lick my fingertips
before turning the page,

And I . . .

I like the sharp intake of your breath
just before Shakespeare hits the floor.

"Navigation"

You caught the moon when it fell.
It turned to a pearl in your hand.
Placed on my tongue,
it dissolved to salt and sweet.
Then, wrapped in constellations
from your head down to your feet,
you commanded me
to navigate
by the stars.

"Meditate"

Birdsong on a chain
rests between my breasts.
It was all that I could save
when I stumbled
on the nest
in flames.

Bible in my bag.
Knife tucked in my boot.
Sowing both sides of the seed.
Both sides taking root,
so I meditate

on inner peace
and payback.

"Love And Affection"

I wanted love
and a little affection.
Baby, you took me
half of the way.

You gave me love
and a little infection.
Goes to show you don't listen
to half of what I say.

"Short Story"

A nice girl settled
for a piece of possible
and died of boredom.

"Blameless"

If it is only a Poem,
then I am Blameless,
no matter the racing of my heart.

I can name this aching Admiration
and be no better or worse
than others who read your verse
and sigh the same.

This flush that stains my cheeks
speaks only to Envy
of your gift so rich and wicked

that it shames my paltry skill
for necessary Fictions.

"The Notes Your Shrink Is Taking"

Pt. appears anxious, reports poor sleep and disturbing dreams.

Some nocturnal activity with amnesia for events.

When asked to more closely examine dream content, pt. begins sporadic tongue click (repetitive behavior: note: non-self injurious: note: emotional conditioning / active amygdala response to memory).

With obvious reluctance, pt. reveals recurring dream of riding naked on a mastodon up a volcano to steal a cherry from a giant rook bearing an uncanny resemblance to his mother.

Freak.

Pick up milk.

"Silence Be Golden"

Please promise me that you will never tell
about that kiss that day down by the well,
the way cool water passed between sweet lips,
or how I yielded to soft fingertips.
Don't whisper of how swiftly virtue fell
with commonsense and camisole as well
to lie forgotten as spring parted me
with words and wondrous tongue so wickedly.
Yes, promise me that you will never tell
about what passed that day down by the well.
For if you do, I shall be forced to claim
to be sinned against . . . and name your name.
So, see silence be golden after all
and never speak a word of what you saw.

"Goddess Suburbia"

My hair is the only hint
that there's a goddess
beneath this ball cap;
not quite gone to crone,
despite the silver strands.

Sheltered in my hollows
is a ripeness
born of doing
and a pearl -
rough wrought -
the blooming
of seven years of sand.

"Roadside Stand"

I
build

bells of bones
and pretty stones
string them for the wind that blows
backwards
east to west
stealing words
stealing sage sweet breath.

I
sell

trinkets
from roadside stands
to catch the eye
and money in hand
of some white man
and his lady;
they don't sleep well at night.

Neither do I.

"Summer Blonde"

I starved myself blonde
that summer.
Wished on every star I saw.
Cluttered the backseat
with boyfriends and girlfriends
and fed myself raven
come fall.

"Animal Girls"

We are laugh eyed dogs
sniffing under logs.
Feeding on the frogs
that failed to prince.
We are alley cats
with a taste for rats
we've caught and crushed flat
in our pawfists.

We are birds of prey
circling through the day.
Seem to fly away . . .
and then we strike.
We're nothing like you.
We're untamed and true.
And, we're gonna do
just as we like.

"What It Was Like"

Outside one morning,
waiting for the bus,
cold
and still half asleep,
I rested my head against a fence post
and my foot on the bottom
strand of wire.

"What are you doin'?"
he hollered from the front porch.
"Nothin',"
I hollered back.

He whipped me twice;
once for having my foot on the wire

and once more for lying about it.

"If We Were Lovers"

If we were lovers,
I would kiss you at red lights-
hard, thoroughly, and unhurriedly-
until cars backed and stacked
and curses blued the air
like vulgar, finely feathered
birds.

*"Green means go
get a fucking room,
why dontcha?"*

I'd lace my fingers with yours,
dangle my feet out the passenger window,
and let you drive me (mad)
to the next intersection.

If we were lovers,
I'd wear your old t-shirts
with heels and with diamonds
and without panties or plans to leave the house
on Saturday night

or Sunday morning.

If we were lovers,
I'd soak in you
like a hot bath

with vanilla lavender bubbles.

"Country Air"

Screams carry clean
through country air,
through unlocked doors, through open windows

when vinegar splashes
sun blistered skin,
and cruelty is the price of being small.

Words warp to starker howls.
Survival strips the curtains down,
and she cocoons

in a makeshift shroud
burning,
burning.

Screams carry clean
through country air.
Lock the doors. Close the windows.

"Places"

I keep my spiders in a jar
and my matches very far
from my gasoline.

I keep my redbirds out of sight
and let my blackbirds fly at night.
When they come back to me,

I ask them what to do with you.

"Be"

I can be your man.

Tall, dark, and handsy.
Magicked up as midnight.
A doorway to the dawn.

I can be your woman.

Brothel born and fancy.
String you south like starlight.
Suck the skin right off your bones.

Don't matter to me
what you want me to be
as long as you be
mine.

I can be your dog.

Panting just to please you.
Roll over on my back
anytime you say.

I can be your cat.

Curling round your legs
and getting all familiar.
Twitch my tail and strut away.

Don't matter to me
what you want me to be
as long as you be
mine.

"Just Friends"

I have a fragment
of full moon
on a chain
and a breathless
beatitude
stained
berry black
on the small of my back -

otherwise, I'd just forget you.

I have a snippet
of verse
in my shoe
and a bottle tree
ready to bloom
between your house and mine.

It straddles the property line

where you end
and I begin -

just friends.

"When He's Gone"

When he's gone,
I take the air
deeper.
I unfold to fill
my natural space.
I reclaim my shadow.

"In Trade"

I'll trade you a kiss
for the key to the cellar.
I hear that there the darkness keeps

its paper dolls
and fractured children,

and I think that I'd feel
more at home there than you.

I'll trade you a kiss
for the leash of the monster.
I hear the rumbling growl in its gut

for paper dolls
and fractured children,

and I think that I'd feed
it far better than you.

I'll trade you a kiss
to lock the door behind me.
I've heard it said that I'm not safe

around paper dolls
and fractured children,

and I fear
that I cannot be trusted with you.

"Camera Eyes"

Fearing that I love you,
I craft camera eyes
to zoom in nearer,
focus clearer;
macro
and magnify.

But, I still
cannot see your insides.

So, fearing that I love you,
I stitch scalpels on my hands
to open you,
explore you;
dissect
and understand.

I'll put you back together
if I can.

"Holy Grounds"

Pilgrims pew to get a view of God;
she never spills the coffee.
Faith is found in holy grounds
held by steady hands.
With the sign of the Sunday crossword,
St. Creola gives each a blessing
and a small to-go-with-God box
as the Queen purrs, "Come again."

"Eccentricities"

I collect my eccentricities
like seashells and bones.
Shine them
till the hollows glow.
Then hold
each one to my ear
to hear oceans all my own.

"Pinwheel Dress"

I was a pigtailed girl
in a pinwheel dress
when Mama met a man
with thigh-high hands
and problems.

There are things you don't talk about.

When I'd balance ballet
across the cattle guard,
he'd peel me like an orange
with his eyes and suck hard
at my segments.

There are things you don't say aloud.

And, I felt so dirty
in my pinwheel dress -
with downcast eyes,
I ran
like I could outrun the mess of me.

There are things I still dream about.

"Garden"

A blood wet thorn shows you
I've been there.
A missing rose means
that I'm gone.

How long
will you try
to deny me
your garden?

My loose latch gate bids you
to enter
and seek the bloom spared
from my shears.

To bring you near,
I appear
to deny you my garden.

"To my Heart"

Wash the dust
from your dusky wings
in the water clock
where every moment brings
another ripple -
a tiny story -

ours.

"Miss D'Meanor"

Call me Miss D'Meanor.
I'm the method and the measure
between the girl who eats the apple
and the girl who bakes the pie.

Never wholly wholesome,
but less than average evil.
Call me Miss D'Meanor;
I'm how the middle makes a life.

"Lightning"

I flew a kite.
I flew a key.
Lightning split the sky
for me.
I boxed it up.
I took it home
so if I should ever be alone

I'd have lightning.

Behind white walls
and a deadbolt door,
I play with lightning
on the floor.
I clap thunder.
I cry rain
until floods come to wash away

all the things I've been fighting

and nothing's left but lightning.

3. POEMS BY JOY ANN JONES

PART ONE: "WITCHLIGHT" 10 LOVE POEMS

"Midnight Riff"

Low low in the midnight
come to dance by the firelight
tune up with that arbitrary grace
substitute sway for that look on your face
in a dark that makes shadow look bright.

Row row over tears
the reedy boat of sprung years
when the shore disappears into mist
that insists you persist don't resist
a distance flung further than fears.

Sole sole is the pathway
burnt bulbs outline the runway
where something much heavier than air
fades away with what made you care;
that departure clocks in the next day.

December 2011

"Oxygen Vine Dreamscape"

a voice was singing

Oxygen vine
sweet life of mine
o how you twine
oxygen vine

You began to turn me leaflike
browsing me in slack moments,
a subscription of yours, a pastime.
I saw a skewed wall in a lunatic jungle,
undeciphered petroglyphs
scrawled over by flaming flower graffiti
dark hands of roots, celladon vineshadows,
utterly unreadable

a nonsense song

Oxygen vine
trace me a line
o how you twine
oxygen vine

I was deaf from the reverberations
 of collision when you told me
I was a wall against whose
resistance you built your self, but
I was only flesh behind a wall
etched with the sigils of an unknown cabal,
 its vines and shadows
become my skin

in the deep night

Oxygen vine
black columbine
o how you twine
oxygen vine

Love is a cannibal you explained.

Gemini / Scorpio / Capricorn

His first goal is to kill and eat the other
then make tuneful bells from the bones.
Just so you grew your tensile intoxicant ribbons in me
so hungry and alive, tickling, strangling
composting accommodating flesh till I was friable ooze
root-fractured, absorbed into your sucking shoots
flensed down to my skull for a drum

sweet notes pulsing

Oxygen vine
razors in wine
o how you twine
oxygen vine

I was wined and twined
cut so quickly
I never knew when my smile lost its lips.
You pierced and numbed me
bubbled my blood out with your own
beads of verdant air, an antagonism of life support
careless of the red drops' splash
or my cyanic throat

rattling and humming

Oxygen vine
ventilator's whine
o how you twine
oxygen vine

Autumn brings a bonfire.
 Dry leaves and twigs burn tinder fast
thorns and flowers flaring farewell
in a temperature that crackles,
twining flames fed hotter
by an inrush of escaping air exploding
black under the lids into
smoke blown like seeds on the wind

vanishing

Oxygen vine

darkness define
your ashen design

into silence

March 2011

"September Storm"

Lightning's not like clouds
full of castles and horses
elephants and eagles;
it's all skinny fishbones
fish hooks and the
skeletons of dragons
lich lightlines walking and
no pouffe at all.

So with you light of my heart;
just a lightning strike against a
shuttered lid.
So with me just a bunch of
dried rosemary
twigging in the wind, so with
love, just a rack of bones to pick
of what once was,

a september
storm
electric sweet still
sighing, sensed, scented
on memory's nightblue fingers.

September 2011

"Morning Coffee at the End Of The Day"

We sat in trance to watch the pale sun rise
drinking chicory coffee whitened with
each others' scents and sighs,
writing poems in the curl of steam
above the cups, chalking on the skies
that spellbright starwild chase that burns the blood
and ends in darkness, quick release, exanimate mud.

"These still must be gobbled down,"
you said, so professorially weird,
grey as grey could be today
in your wooly suit and beard.
All was not as well as hoped, but much as feared,
for loving is the gate I can't pass by
and being loved a knot I'll never tie.

I'm not afraid to keep these mocha kisses,
or braid a supple rope of words
to belt a habit culled from misses,
but what are you, which ghost do I love now?
Even as I ask, the heart confesses:
You love the thing that always runs before,
the shadow come to howl at heaven's door.

Yet still we drink our coffee here and sing,
those songs that suit our joint imagining;
all bits of you blown scattered across the years,
each artifact dug from bone and cleaned with tears;
the amber eyes, the brown, the sailor blue,
the crack of wise, the note that's always true,
the bridge that builds itself from golden air,

while you sip, and morning softly greys your hair
from yellow, currant black, till nothing's there.

August, 2011

"The Scout"
(For the Man Who Told Me Never To Write Down His Name)

Back when I was lost
I loved you, the pathfinder
alone among men known to
disarm the plaint of the frog sentinels,
and allowed to pass the trees' seedlings
covered in their rustling beds, soundless,
walking like a snowflake over the breasts
of sleeping wrens,
sent to pull me from
the ooze and gel of the mire.

You did
but what a cost.
You lost your beaded moccasins,
your pipe and pelts, your mule.
I lost my pain only to see it
found in a new spot,
coming up like the weed it is
needing always to be pulled.
You moved on to another frontier

of lost but far from fallow women,
scouting out that ever expanding horizon.
I think you walk there still, quick and
soft as the memory of a
leaf that never falls.

November 2010

"Incubus"

Late at night
when sleep's a joke
told for hours without a punchline
the incubus comes by.

It's a wild
but comforting thing; the horns
hardly show and it knows
how to make the tail
so useful
but sometimes
the goat eye slants
and pins me to the bed,
the cleft foot
burns where it walks
on my chest;
but still

I laugh like a fool
for the nights
you come to me, brined with
memory, slick with salt.

June 2011

"Blue Masque"

We took a break from the butcher's ballet
to dance a few steps where the bank met
the whittling river.
You wore your blue mask, your milky skin,
your matchbook eyes
umber and ruminant.

They lamped the meadow,
illuminant for all the wayward
menagerie of my fancy

Shay Caroline Simmons, Kelli Simpson, Joy Ann Jones

there in the black
New England midnight
when the fireflies began to burn.

Your cloak your russet hair in dark folds stippled your face
that day, the day before I cut it for the road. It
hung the shadow in my eyes, blew like dying stars
on the long wind, snapped across the night
to catch in my lips, give them a taste
of salt surprise and you a veil

for the look you always had to blur.
The balefires burned while the world hissed and spat
nowhere near that shingle of void where we kissed.
Lives came and went, the planets placed a pirouette
rippling in your face that showed only
the crabshell mirror of the halfmoon's smile.

The whispered words, the sentient fingers
flicked lingering on my stops so much more
fluently than on your instrument of brass,
the reed of my desire that ever bent between
your tongue and will, all of me you caused
to make that music never heard on stage;

the truth that spilled like blood,
the plangent harmonics
beyond the bordered breaths,
the sighs, the cries, the tears
coming to us unseen
walking on the riptide of the years;

that was the blue masque we made
the music we played there before you blazed.
Then, while the bonfires of war
burned brighter and the mill
of the gods
ground small.

April 2011

"Deadlight"

We walked together, your fetch and I
under a dry black moon
in a milk wet sky.

I talked at length to what had no ear.
Dead light crunched underfoot
in the burning of the year.

To all I asked, its cloud lips were sealed
and its star eyes were filmed
to blank white wheels.

It had no more breath, no more words than a stone
but yet it was better
than walking alone.

"Deadlight Redux"
In Cyhydedd Hir Form

We walked together
in black moon weather
your fetch and I under a milk wet sky.

I talked, each word dear
to what had no ear
in the burning year, under dead light.

Its cloud lips were sealed
its blank eyes white wheels
all I asked, it peeled from my own sighs.

It had no more home,
no more words than stone
yet walking alone's hard by dead light.

August 2012

"Vessel"

When the moon
is winking
like the Grey Sisters' eye
passed from housetop
to housetop, glassy bright
and wide as a fawn's
I feel your touch

the wind in the night
cool on fever's summer,
you who can kiss with the taste
of rain and break the drought,
your look slips my skin
wet and terra cotta slick
as the clay on the wheel.

Run your potter's hand
across my back
reshape my nights, my days
with lover's fingers
pliant as willow.
Fire me where the blaze
burns white.

Paint me with
bard's colors
blue as the high july sky
rosy, yellow, crimson
with every flower
then take me to the well
where thirst is quenched.

September 2011

"Incubus: Finale"

The incubus struggles
with depression,

reluctantly fulfilling
the contract,
turning his bitches
over to
Beelzebub.

He broods.
All
that brimstone
acrobatic
badass act
for
nothing.

August 2012

PART 2. "CASTING THE RUNES"
SPELLS, MYTHS AND LEGENDS.

"Odin's day Night"

I wrap a poor turn
of grizzled hope
around the moon
so frayed
I wrap it in the too
opulent velvet
of a voice
so dark
singing the
old

sagas of inamoratas
journeys' endings
rhymes of baldur's fall
monks' canted fragments
figments of
gods and demons
queens and fools
past and future
love and death.

The night sky is freckled
with perseid's white splash,
droplets of star burning
strained through the alembic
of a staring nullity
defining my preterition,
sizzling like the rasp
of some old god's laugh
rough from a silence
passing paleology.

How their light runs
fleet suns of Perseus
skittering across

night's spread table
a howl on the ripped nail
of moon splintering

on Odin's day
night as remote
as the face behind
a blue electric vow,
close as
the corvine quark
tumbling sable japes.

That laughter in the air,
yelling from the beaks of crows
falls high above

beyond the circling light;
how the void must ring with it
time out of mind
in perpetuum.

August 2011

"Nereid"

She came to me
because with bell book and candle
she was cast out, alone
with her wand of basil and stars.
She stroked my hand, wrapped me round
in words of a tongue I could not speak.
She stood naked before me
hairless and smooth as bone
an offering I had no use for
and I was sad for her wildness
that could find no home on this earth
except in the fretful dreams of
the starving.

October 3, 2011

"Viking Funeral"

I haven't seen you since
the viking funeral when
all the boat was burning and
you were the dog at my feet.

The wind is in the east
and my old wounds ache;
the line of scar across my
fingers, almost severed

when you drew on me
for touching,
won't stop throbbing, and though
they were embossed on my shield

against my will
the ice age,
the broken lands
are now my own.

I drowse when I can in the sun
outside Sleipnir's stable,
where Ceridwen's cauldron
leans ready against the wall,

deaf to Loki making
a bloodwar fuss over Sif's shorn hair
the yapping liar's mouth
unfaithful, untrue.

The memory of heat
on still red scars
soothes, burning all
alike to ash,

black bones of deceit,
the cur at my feet.

April 2012

Gemini / Scorpio / Capricorn

"the jazzman gets the blues"

the jazzman came to Wyandotte
he was lookin to play.
he had his axe in a worn out case
looked like it had been pissed on
by a thousand dogs--
black, peeling, no stickers--
and a bone box with a
beating heart
in his back pocket.

the jazzman found a corner by the bus station
where the winos were huffin it up
from a paper bag.
decided it looked like a place that
needed accompaniment,
so he took out his sax and made a noise like a combine
on a july day in Longview.
the winos left.

an old latina woman on her way to work
threw a quarter in his case
out of pity.

the jazzman left Wyandotte
because he'd paid his dues
and hitched to the West Coast.
he had some money left
but he let the
truckers and salesmen
feed him anyway.

he finally made it to L.A.
and cast the hairy eyeball around.
he was wiped out and freakin,
needed bong hits and bedrest.
he was lookin to get laid.

he did.

scroungin a gig was harder

but he hooked up with a whacked out bass player
from Fargo who made everybody call him Fats
two hipsters with guitars
and a rastafarian on the conga.
they called the band the Lounge Lizards.
they played Manny's Chuck House every Friday
for two months.
the jazzman thought his chops
were finally there.

then the waitress Manny was boppin
ran off with all his bread, and Fats.
Manny went flat busted and got kidney trouble.
The one guitar player's old lady had him
thrown in the slammer
for ten years' child support
and the other went mariachi in Tiajuana.
the rastafarian kept playin the conga
but it was no good, man.

the jazzman was frosted.
he had to agitate the gravel.
he left L.A. thinkin about Wyandotte.
he still had his axe and his dogpiss case
but he was runnin low on reeds
and he thought he might be
gettin the blues.

there was a flick at the time--
it was bitchin, about Death Stars.
it razzed the jazzman's berries.
he knew he needed a schtick, so he kyped a violin,
got the vader threads, and learned to hiss and wheeze.
he wrote a song called "I'm your big daddy-o, Luke baby."
it bombed.

so the jazzman hit the road
for the last time.
he thought he met Keruac once
outside an old diner in St Paul
but it was just a shadetree mechanic
named Dwayne. he never made it back
to Wyandotte and he lost

the bone box with the beating heart
somewhere just north of Burns Flat
when he got those hellhound blues, Clyde,
really bad.

February 2011

"Bonedancer"

Bonedancer, hear me.
I sing the song
that burns the candle
here beside the flume of dark
where Styx meets bright Tiger
where Persephone falters
eating one sweet seed after another
too long too dry to stop.

Bonedancer, fly
in the dream I dream
of the totem wolf talking
of skinshifters walking
where the waking's hard
but the sleeping is harder
on memory's cold stones,
loser's bloat and bones.

Bonedancer, pivot
above the look
that shakes a threshing
from a sowing
that calls to its own
on strings of wild
violin eyes, hiss
your mother bird's chorus, chuffling
your chicks towards a white sun
candle that burns in the grass.

November 2012

"Death of the Doll"

I knew when I sold him the doll,
took her from her spellwrought womblight
and felt the hard silver in my hand,
everything changed.

Her soft cloth body wrinkled its rayon ribs,
shuddered all its length.
Her scarab eyes, turquoise beads in black,
stared dead flowers then blinked.

She knew
every secret
and I knew
she'd be made to tell.

They came soon, the droning
gibbering buzzardy crew
full of the code she told
within my bones, the flashing

white sigils of my wrists
the deep bleeding where I hid
the treacherous river in the skullcave
that wheels Leibniz's reversible mill.

They were there before me
at every hole; behind me as I ran
came the breath, the slap and flap
the assassin's cautious laugh

muffled

when the blade crossed my throat.
I could not blame her,
she whose stuffing filled the air and drained
down the front
of my cotton chest.

November 2012

"Stormcrow"

Stormcrow
catch me if you can.
Circle and dive as I collapse
in a brick arpeggio,
shattering harpsichord ice bells.
Blow the thaw jazzed as a discord
down from the burning brass horn
of your craw.
Set your ebonyblue wings acrawl, wind
moonpock shadows on my shoulders,
your gaze a crackling smoke
of black wildflowers
flamed in the wickered willow
of your yellow eye.

Stormcrow
weep me out another winter
after the fall. I've been waiting,
rebuilding my broken bone box
here in your cold penumbra,
seen how you
cock your too cunning head,
pretend to pace on crooked toes, seen
how you love hovering high
showing one crescent feather of
a starbead-bright galaxy, hiding the
brush of full dark; still
I know tomorrow you'll catch me
if you can, my stormcrow
if you can.

January 2013

"Freyja Speaks To The Skalds"

Now I call you, brother
across the ticking void.
Feel my hand in yours,
over the scars and tears.
I'm with you where you sit
milling the weary hours
finer finer into a dry flour
that chokes the heart's pores
for its bitter bread

as I was with you
when you raised the promise-cup
in Midgard's torch-red halls
and played for swinish ears
that ragged tune
of stars and battles, destinies of glass
of ebbing tides and the bones
of love's last child, with
the gods' last dance

there before
we wore our names,
when your hand spiraled
deep in the womb black cave,
lining for me the ochre herds
wallrunning to fill the stomach
of evernight with life
for all eternity's migration.
I held you up

in your thin skin boat
of fancy's faith and grief;
I tried you, through the floods
of high seas' anchorage,
through the dark blood conquest,
holding the dripping blade. In
the stone-ringed grove
under the crooked moon
I spared your life,

left you one-eyed, lamed but singing
in a tinsel of smudged neon night
on a winedark streetcorner wave
where every loss collides
in subway clamor or benched
in garden's dusky still. For you my
pole-circling breath melts and blows
the spice of far Carib, because
I call you brother.

Under threads of silver gold
where seven shed skins make
a thorny crossroads of your face
still you vigil for the heartsong.
Hear my fade note whisper on shadow wind:
call me, call me, always I will come
but when the sun pours through
white curtains and every
bell is ringing

of course the spell
is broken and
I'm gone.

February-March 2012

"Scapegoat"

Don't go near that girl, the old women cried.
Her slant-eyed look
dried her mother's milk;
sister died.
There's something wrong inside.
She's dangerous.

Yes, now--
changeling child of lies.

~October, 2012

"Circe Speaks"

After twenty-six cups of wine
A warrior turns into a swine.
They called it witch's sorcery, poison lore;
But really, all I ever did was pour.

August 2012

"Feeding The Plumed Serpent"

The day after our wedding with the moon
in the piercing sun of a blood drinking god
we rode back through dust on the rocking bus
shy dark children patting, taking my yellow hair
for lizard feathers. They turned off Madonna and
you sang their songs. They laughed your laugh
each one the child we'd never have.
We went back to the slum hotel and locked the door
while the drunks hurricaned up and down the halls;
we the same up and down the walls, the stairs, the
fretted sheets, up one belly and down the other

till we were drunk as they could never be
and saw the things no seer ever could say.

When your body moved on mine in neon glare
it was the black shadow and white light
of that pyramid of skulls and jaguar's caves
where amaranthine sacrifice filled
death's new toybox, blood for lubricant
easing the clockwork bones,
throats craned toward the copper knife,
your dark eyes swimming with night
carving into timeblurred petroglyphs
my life upon their lids, feathered cries
vapor murmured out in velvet visions,

spinning down down

into the solstice of light and dark.

In the cold morning we drank atole hot and sweet
with all the vanilla thickness of my flesh
against your whipcord bones a steam
rising remembered in each sip.
Your thin musician's hands held the cup
in mimic of the circling of my breasts
stroked to purrs and sweat on the hard bed.
Oh, having me for breakfast was
the richest meal you ever bought
and paid for with
each drop of the god's owned blood

until time came
to put the toys away.

January 2012

"Rán's Road"

"...With fearful might the sea surged
Methinks our stems the clouds cut,-
Rán's road to the moon soared upward..."
~The Prose Edda

Back home
from nowhere
on the sundown road again
out beyond the ending
after the wildest wave,
a light floods
sunfallen scarlet in seastream.

Feeling stops, mind in
memory's mooring
no longer finds netted
maritime eyes of pearl
rippling sundrops
chained shells of silver
to barnacle the heart.

Still, far inland
a spring wells
dripping from the split rock
a dribble, compared to that
vast redstained road flowing
from white Rán's mouth, yet
quenching, sweet not salt;
time stops the oarsmen,
the twin bladed hands
are still in the dark.

Alone becomes
a mooncell, it's centromere
suspended, each joining
separating identical
chromotids, a whole
from division's drilled duality
a sensate totality
light made from shadow.

When
the soul returns
from her long journey
impossible not to know her
under the silver hair
the shabby close
the smile unchanged.

"...The stormy breast rain-driven,
The wave with red stain running,
Out of white Rán's mouth..."
~Ibid.

December 2011

"A Remedy For Memory"

Walking widdershins,
wind your vine around the
headstone of a first wife
dead in childbed.
Let the gourd increase over graveyard
grass, watered with the grey cloudwine
of starless night.

When the fruit is full, scoop out
the innards, then pierce it a mouth with
the sharpened legbone of
an old doe who
stumbled at the last ditch.
Let this dry in October sun.

Meanwhile,
take the howl of a midnight train
three sparrow feathers, nine grains of skypollen
from a falling star, six tears from
a drunkard's melancholic fit.
Mix with the scent of last summer's promises
and a cupful of nettle's milk, well

pounded with a fist of stone in a
hollowed heart. Fill your gourd with this liquor,
bury it at the crossroads for seven weeks, then
exhume it and drink deep
under an extinguished moon.
It may be then
you will forget him.

Should this cordial fail you,
marry the butcher.

~September 2012

"In Hel's Hall"

It was white-ice morning in Hel's Hall
in the ninth of the Nine Worlds, when
Odin donned the Hel-shoes, cast the runes
and rode to ask his questions of
the dead.

Because he was a god, twisted she rose
from her ashen bed
and by force began to speak
of what she knew:

So I found, said the blackened lips,
that cold is a serpent that holds, pushing its
ribbon-chest deep into mountain,
slow-cracking the heads of the spirits within
for gold to brighten its rippling scales.
Will you hear more?

So I saw, moved the fleshless jaw,
cold grow wide and thicken,
putting on its grey-white armor,
that its dead mouth kisses every shoulder,
that the tree it circles
will shake down a harvest of lives
to grind out all you love.

So I found, rattled the dustdry throat,
that cold will make red daggers, hanging
scarlet borrowed blood to temper
oblivion's poppy snowflakes,
to pierce the heart of hearts
till red and white alike
vanish from sight.

So I saw, whispered the husk of Hel,
that snow will cover fire,
that the white wolf no sword can kill
will eat desire, that you
are a basket of bones made for wildflowers
withering in a wind of empty hours.
Will you hear more?

Then the One-Eyed shucked his Hel-shoes
jumped back in Sleipnir's saddle,
and fled the Ninth World,
where the wisdom he begged
had frozen on his tongue.

~January 2013

PART 3. "DANCING DOLL"   An Assortment Of Form Poems.

"Red Shoes"
A Rondel

She danced through the night. Her shoes were red.
She rang her bell of tulle and ribbons, dress of dreams.
The master cued her moves and sewed her seams
and made her body over like a doll's without a head.

He chorcographed her *pas de deux*, a masque of the dead.
She must be only air, her bones hollow as moonbeams.
She danced through the night. Her shoes were red,
stiff her bell of tulle and ribbons, dress of dreams,

She danced through the night. Her shoes were red,
though cream when she began the final themes.
She rang her bell of tulle and ribbons, dress of dreams.
Violins bowed the razor while she bled.
She danced through the night, her shoes were red.

January 2011

"Tale of the Nine-Tailed Fox"
A Terza Rima

There is a fox, a kitsune cunning,
prowling the world I'm dreaming unbound.
No hunter on earth can keep up with his running.

He hides and he smiles. He seldom is found.
His feet are soft sheathes for his adamant claws.
My fox has dark wisdom and tails that abound.

In the east he's a seer on fleet spirit paws.
In the west he's a trickster of convivial drifts.
In the snow he's ice white until the world thaws.

Sometimes he's a she, a vixen who shape shifts,
who marries or buries her blind mortal spouse,
leaves a pup or a throat-bite and takes the man's gifts,

but always in dreams there's a fox in my house.
Remote like all wild things from pity's remorse,
my skin is his shelter, my heart his caught mouse.

My hounds all pursue him but can't stay the course.
The red-coated Hunt fast becomes a wild rout
where dog falls on dog, and the fox beats the horse.

In his covert of flesh he hides safe from the clout,
then he grows a new tail and chews his way out.

December 2010

"Sweetener"
A Triptych
(form courtesy of Kerry O'Connor)

I.

I put you in my tea
tannic with memories;
stirred, they go down smoother
sipping on your ways.
Put on my plate you make
an evergreen presentation,
dressed in rue and fired clay,
so haute cuisine, salad of baby greens
tossed in hope and fear, before
the soup of dreams.

II.
I put you on the moon
sitting where she bends
your cloven feet a-dangle in
their blurred and slippery stars.
You ease Orion's belt, give cloudy listening blinks;
I whisper in your thunder covered ear until
you put me in the storm
flying with wings of rain
where cold front meets the warm.

III.

I put you in my heart
little shop of horrors
cobweb seeded, only one
flyblown object on display but not
for sale. Pressed against the glass
your firefly face winks in the indigo night
where ribboned time slips tight in a lover's knot
and tea is sweet as your blue sky mouth my love,
sweeter than floating memories dead in the pot.

March 2012

"Night Thing"
A Clarian Sonnet

I see that I've become a night thing now,
that even lust burns out, both song and vow.
When candles gutter down too many times,
when stuttering love has used up all her rhymes,
when darkness sucks out colors' hoarded breath;
then I the night thing learn the face of death.
I even put it on to try the fit;
so tight, so stiff, but I've grown used to it.
I take it off when daylight pales the sky
but find it needful under night's ink eye.
Two dogs and I come haunt this vacant lawn
where two fires burned but one of them is gone.
The mouse cries shrill and then the barnowl hoots.
Age clicks the thirty eight before she shoots.

May 2012

"Flash And Thunder"
A Nonet/Reverse Nonet

Flash and thunder can't break the panes in
the hothouse I keep at heart's core
where you're centered in my cells
moonflower on fire
where no careless-shut
door can let in
a flash of
killing
frost.

Frost
curdles
as sure as
fire consumes
or flood waters drown
but who wouldn't plead for
quick burning over a soaked
sponge of lung or the long white death,
stiff in winter's numbing arms alone.   (March 2012)

"Hedgerider's Lament"
A Yule Sestina

It's the time when amber green light soaks the sponge of mist,
dripping softly where worlds rub shoulders in vast night,
dreaming in the nest where brown eggs shift and crackle in the air,
where I'm looking, looking, hearing soundless bells in the blue.
The grass bends, the sparrows talk, and magic guards this place
as I edge myself along the walls of the razorleafed hedgerow.

I see them all, patient, living, bent to purpose in the hedgerow
waiting where the edges are sharp, or under the amber green mist.
Horehound lolls silver tongues, mint droops, amanita puts in place
red spotted chairs for sprites and roofs for toadlings. Shadow night
hides monkshood in its cobalt cap, telling me something fatally blue,
and ladyslippers wait for mousewomen where foxgloves dot the air.

My skull is a tangling rootball of hair and bone and air.
My skin is ambergreen bark against the razorleaves of the hedgerow.
My eyes are storm clouds flickering outwards, grey and blue.
My rabbit nose is twitching, pink in the dripping mist,
breathing in and out, sifting and shaking the smells from the night,
passing hands above the edges, feeling leaves for the right place.

I see a medicine fire drifting the air with grey, burning in the place
where a fallen piece of star has struck a match against hard air,
making sage smoke and sweetgrass smolder in the night,
like tobacco in the pipes of gnomes carousing in the hedgerow.
Other nights I lift a glass, beg them wash their beards in mist
but tonight I cannot stop to joke for the place is near, so cold and blue.

I can hear the worlds go sloshing in their shells, spinning in the blue
almost touching, noses pushing membranes towards the place
where the new year sleeps in the old year's arms, damp with mist
and the quick bear the dead upon their backs, howling thru air
sharp silenced by what dwells just past the hedgerow
because the time is not quite yet, though it nears in the shortening night.

Day has sighed and gone, spent from matching itself to night
so perfectly. My hair jigs up in Tesla's dance, jumping white & blue.

I feel them creeping, riding the top of the razored hedgerow
where it's thin as my skin. Now all but my hair is frozen in place.
Burnt tumbled smells, the soft horse muzzle of the night air
nudges them at me, while at last the steelsharp leaves begin to mist.

Now I can see you blur and move, in mist waves of ribboned night.
I reach out to the air. There where the thorns have turned blue
is the place I can pull you from your lost world, thru the hedgerow.

~December 2010

---

4. ONE FORM, THREE POETS

A CASCADE POEM
BY EACH OF THE AUTHORS

"House Amid The Lupines" by Shay Caroline

Two wolves with but three eyes between them
set each half its teeth in my heart;
having given such rare food to feed them,
it killed me to tear them apart.

The shepherd with spectacles woolen,
was convinced he certainly dreamed them;
while his damned bloody blindness emboldened
two wolves with but three eyes between them.

As Mistress, I sanctioned the pasture
for concealing the Moon and the Stars;
but the Sun, in league with the Master,
set each half its teeth in my heart.

The cook baked her devils some sheep's heads
from her oven she built in the deep den;
then she served herself with their sweetbreads,
having given such rare food to feed them.

My wolfish love with the Master
set hooks through the meat of our hearts;
when our opposite tempers tugged faster,
it killed me to tear them apart.

"Darkling / Old Suns Die" by Kelli Simpson

There is a garden
where blackness blooms
and old suns die.

Where seeds of stardust stilled
hold the last of light.
There is a garden

in the crescent of the moon.
I sheave its shadows
where blackness blooms.

And, last, I tend the darkling child -
as time bends back
and old suns die.

"Rain In The Night" by Joy Ann Jones

I hear it raining, raining tonight
or is it the singing of water
that everything empty be filled,
effulgent, if only with tears?

High up comes the shadowy spinner
to wind up the wandering flood,
to weave away yesterday's orphans;
I hear it raining, raining tonight.

A storm sent to midwife disaster
turns the howl of the wind in its womb,
brings wildfire and blood to the birthing
or is it the singing of water

dropping in petticoats of ash
dappling the mirror faced border?
The lightning-struck bodies on fire
let everything empty be filled

thinking that which is broken and battered
can be smoothed into glimmering bits
shining rounded and faithfully polished,
if only by infinite tears.

February 2013

FIND SHAY CAROLINE AT

SHAY'S WORD GARDEN

HTTP://FIREBLOSSOM-WORDGARDEN.BLOGSPOT.COM

FIND KELLI SIMPSON AT

ANOTHER DAMN POETRY BLOG

HTTP://MAMANEEDSSHOES.BLOGSPOT.COM

FIND JOY ANN JONES AT

VERSE ESCAPE

HTTP://VERSISCAPE-LIFESENTENCES.BLOGSPOT.COM

ABOUT THE AUTHORS

Shay Caroline Simmons is a mail lady who lives in Michigan and enjoys reading, cooking, and listening to Emmylou Harris.

Kelli Simpson is a stay at home mom who lives in Oklahoma. She likes football, Law & Order, and, of course, new shoes.

Joy Ann Jones also lives in Oklahoma, is married, and likes to watch political shows and kill zombies on her computer.

This is their first book.

www.ingramcontent.com/pod-product-compliance
Lightning Source LLC
Chambersburg PA
CBHW060807050426
42449CB00008B/1581